ORIGAMI
FOR FUN!

By Thiranut Deborah Berry

Content Adviser: June Sakamoto, OrigamiUSA, New York City, New York
Reading Adviser: Frances J. Bonacci, Ed.D., Reading Specialist, Cambridge, Massachusetts

COMPASS POINT BOOKS
MINNEAPOLIS, MINNESOTA

Compass Point Books
3109 West 50th Street, #115
Minneapolis, MN 55410

Visit Compass Point Books on the Internet at www.compasspointbooks.com
or e-mail your request to custserv@compasspointbooks.com

Illustrator: Anotoine Clarke and Mie Tsuchida/Bill SMITH STUDIO
Artist: Benjamin Leslie

Editors: Deb Berry and Aubrey Whitten/Bill SMITH STUDIO; and Shelly Lyons
Designer/Page Production: Geron Hoy, Kavita Ramchandran, Sinae Sohn, Marina Terletsky, and Brock Waldron/Bill SMITH STUDIO
Photo Researcher: Jacqueline Lissy Brustein, Scott Rosen, and Allison Smith/Bill SMITH STUDIO
Art Director: Jaime Martens
Creative Director: Keith Griffin
Editorial Director: Carol Jones
Managing Editor: Catherine Neitge

Illustrator: Mie Tsuchida and Antoine Clarke/Bill SMITH STUDIO
Artist: Ben Froikin

Library of Congress Cataloging-in-Publication Data
Berry, Thiranut Deborah.
  Origami for fun! / by Thiranut Deborah Berry.
       p. cm. -- (For fun!)
  Includes bibliographical references and index.
  ISBN 0-7565-1689-7 (hard cover)
 1. Origami. I. Title. II. Series.
  TT870.B4675 2005
  736'.982--dc22
                        2005030283

Table of Contents

The Basics

INTRODUCTION/Origami for Everyone!............4

HISTORY/Folding Formal to Fun 6

ORIGAMI PAPER/Which Paper to Use 8

UNDERSTANDING DIAGRAMS/Follow the Directions .10

BASIC FOLDS/Mountains and Valleys 12

Doing It

SIMPLE ORIGAMI BASES/Covering Your Bases 14

PROJECT #1/The Snake 16

PROJECT #2/The Masu Box 18

PROJECT #3/Origami Photo Album..............20

PROJECT #4/The Samurai Helmet...............22

PROJECT #5/The Boat........................24

PROJECT #6/The Cicada 26

MULTIPLE-PIECE ORIGAMI/Making a Scene 28

People, Places, and Fun

SHARING PATTERNS/Pass the Paper..............30

ORIGAMI BY CHILDREN/ For Kids Only! 32

ORIGAMI FOR PEACE/ 1,000 Cranes 34

PAPER WORLDS/Welcome to Oriland!.............36

COMPLEX ORIGAMI/It's All in the Math! 38

FAMOUS FOLDERS/Who's Made History in Origami?40

TIMELINE/What Happened When? 42

TRIVIA/Fun Origami Facts 44

• •

QUICK REFERENCE GUIDE/Origami Words to Know.46

GLOSSARY/Other Words to Know.................47

WHERE TO LEARN MORE.......................47

INDEX.....................................48

Note: In this book, there are two kinds of vocabulary words. Origami Words to Know are words specific to origami. They are defined on page 46. Other Words to Know are helpful words that aren't related only to origami. They are on page 47.

Origami for Everyone!

Have you ever noticed that when you have a piece of paper in your hand, you want to fold it almost by instinct? We've all done this with a sheet of notebook paper or a dollar bill. You might not realize it, but every time you fold paper, you are doing origami. The word *origami* is the Japanese term for "paper folding." Each time you fold a letter to put into an envelope, or a note to put in your pocket, it's origami!

Most people think of origami as a Japanese art form, but there are origami enthusiasts and organizations in many countries. As new paper folders emerge with each new generation, origami continues to develop and grow.

Folding Formal to Fun

Japanese culture is known for its beautiful simplicity. Even food preparation is considered an art form in Japan. Paper folding is just another way the Japanese pay tribute to life's simpler pleasures and beauty.

The word *origami* is Japanese, but it is uncertain whether paper folding started in China or Japan. Paper was invented in China in 105 A.D. but did not make its way to Japan until around 610. Little is known about the early days of paper folding in Japan, but from 794 to 1868, the elite classes used creative paper folding for letters and gift wrapping. By the 1960s, origami started to become extremely popular in the West.

10,000 Cranes and Counting

In Japan, school children fold thousands of cranes. Cranes symbolize happiness, peace, longevity, and good health. Folding the cranes demonstrates the power of unity and their hope for world peace.

Which Paper to Use

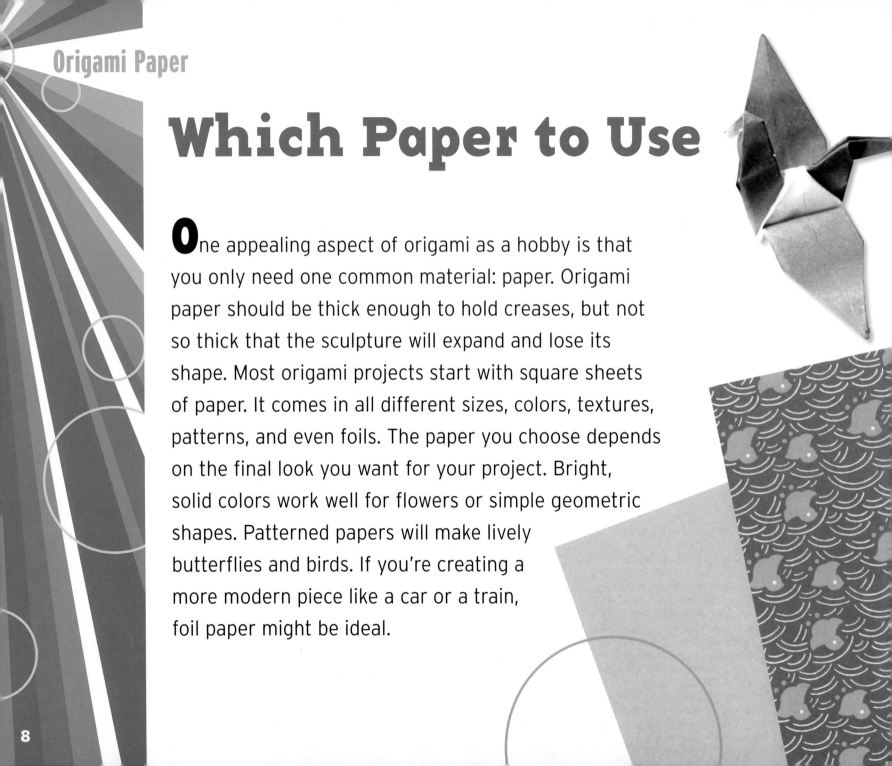

One appealing aspect of origami as a hobby is that you only need one common material: paper. Origami paper should be thick enough to hold creases, but not so thick that the sculpture will expand and lose its shape. Most origami projects start with square sheets of paper. It comes in all different sizes, colors, textures, patterns, and even foils. The paper you choose depends on the final look you want for your project. Bright, solid colors work well for flowers or simple geometric shapes. Patterned papers will make lively butterflies and birds. If you're creating a more modern piece like a car or a train, foil paper might be ideal.

Most craft, stationery, and book stores stock papers made for origami. If you're just starting and don't want to use fancy paper for practice, start with plain white paper. You can also cut standard white computer paper into squares. It's a good idea to practice any design on inexpensive paper before you try it on the paper you want for the final piece.

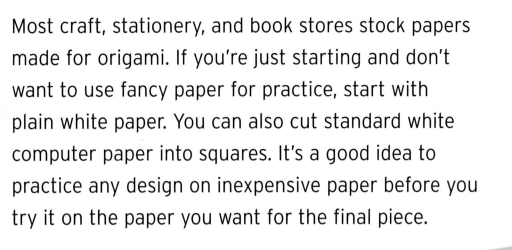

Irogami for Origami

Origami paper known as *irogami* is white on one side and colored or patterned on the other. You can make your own irogami using ordinary wrapping paper. Folded wrapping paper is easier to work with than the rolled kind. For either type, use a ruler or a cardboard cutout to outline a square on the white side of the paper. Then cut the square out of the paper.

Follow the Directions

One reason that origami has become universally popular is that diagrams are drawn in a universal language. The symbols used in origami diagrams are the same regardless of the language. This is important since many origami diagrams come with little or no written instruction.

The first time you try to read an origami diagram, you might feel baffled. It's easy to be confused by all the lines, dashes, arrows, and other symbols. The key is to focus on one diagram at a time and one symbol at a time. Try using an extra sheet of paper to cover the diagrams that you're not using.

Once you've done enough projects, understanding origami diagrams will become second nature.

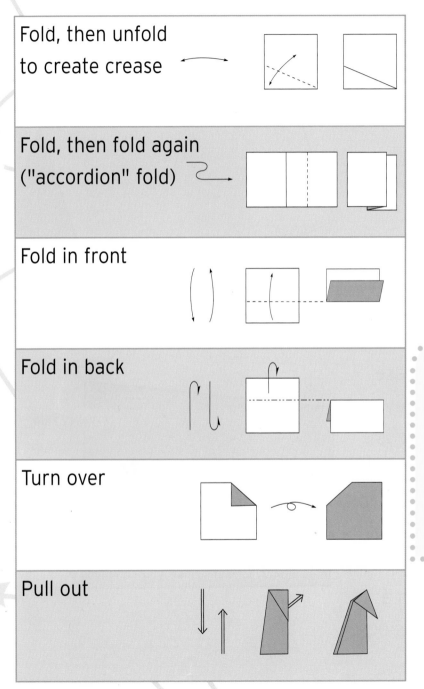

Fold, then unfold
to create crease

Fold, then fold again
("accordion" fold)

Fold in front

Fold in back

Turn over

Pull out

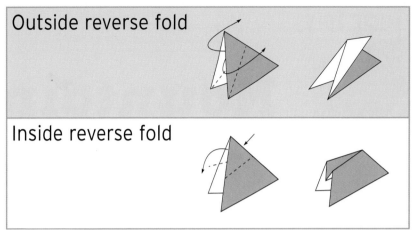

Outside reverse fold

Inside reverse fold

Valley-fold line	– – – –	lets you know when to create a valley.
Mountain-fold line	–·–·–·–·	lets you know when to create a mountain.
Crease line	———	shows you where a crease will be
X-ray line	··············	shows you what paper looks like on the inside.

Mountains and Valleys

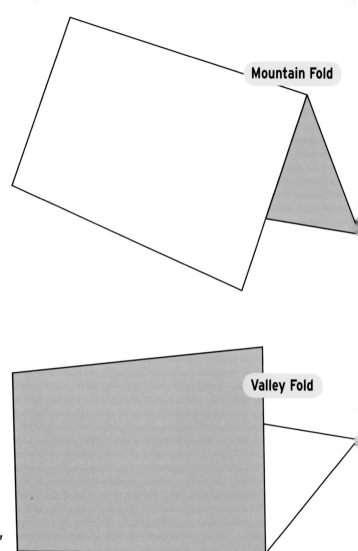

Mountain Fold

Valley Fold

The two most basic folds in any origami project are mountains and valleys. Both terms actually refer to the same crease. Whether the crease is considered a mountain or a valley depends on whether the color side is facing in or out. If you fold the top half of a sheet toward yourself, you have made a valley. If you fold it away, you have a mountain. Also, with a valley fold, the colored side is facing out. With a mountain fold, the white side faces out.

Mountain Fold:

For a mountain fold, with the white side facing you, fold the top of the paper away from you.

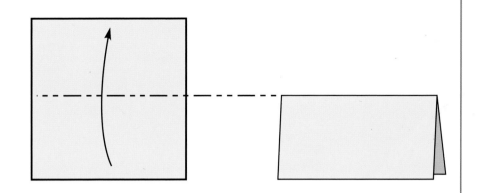

Valley Fold:

For a valley fold, with the white side facing you, fold the top of the paper toward you.

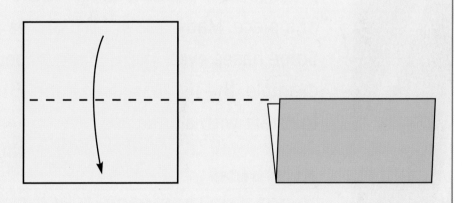

More Basic Folds

Other basic folds include the petal, rabbit ear, squash, crimp, pleat, sink, inside reverse, and outside reverse. Learning the basic folds of origami will help you follow instructions and diagrams and even create your own designs as your folding skills get better.

Covering Your Bases

For a beginner, bases are a great starting point to practice your paper folding. A base forms the start of a piece. Many origami sculptures start with a base. Some bases even instruct you to begin with a base. For example, the fish base (see page 15) instructs the folder to "start with a kite base."

Kite base

1. Fold paper in half diagonally, then unfold.	
2. Fold in the two sides to align with the center crease.	

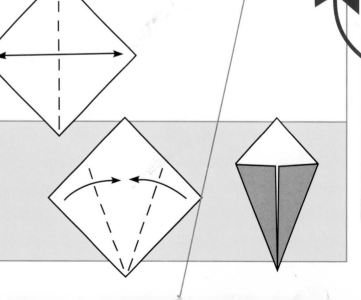

Fish base

1. Start with a kite base (see page 14), and with the open folded side face down, fold the bottom point up to meet the top point.

2. Turn it over.

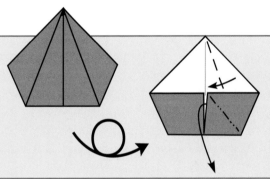

3. Pull each corner out and downward, folding the paper's edge inward to meet the center line.

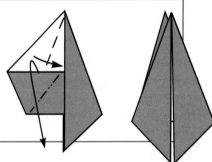

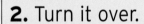

A more complex base is the fish base. This base starts with the simple kite base.

15

The Snake Out of the Grass

These pretty serpents don't hiss or bite! The diamond-patterned snake is one of the simplest origami sculptures to fold, too. For this project, you'll need to use irogami paper. You can also use paper that is one color or pattern on one side, and another on the other side. Both sides of the paper have to be different to get the visual effect.

1. With the color side facing up, fold the paper corner to corner to create a crease, then unfold.

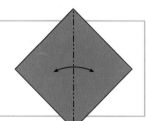

2. Fold each corner over and over toward the center crease so you end up with seven equally spaced creases on each side of the center crease. Unfold, then alternate mountain and valley folds along the creases you created.

3. Mountain fold the body of the snake, lengthwise, while at the same time valley folding the neck.

4. Fold down the head.

5. Fold over the tongue.

6. Make alternate mountain and valley folds to curl the body of the snake.

The Masu Box

You can use origami to create useful objects, such as wallets, bags, boxes, and CD covers. One popular origami sculpture is the masu box. The Japanese word *masu* refers to a small wooden box used to measure rice or beans. In origami, small paper boxes can be folded to hold all kinds of goodies, from candy to jewelry.

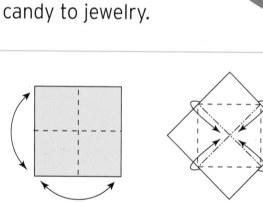

1. With the colored side up, fold the paper in half, left over right, then unfold. Fold the paper in half, top over bottom, then unfold.

2. With the colored side down, fold all four corners in to meet the center point.

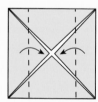

3. Fold the left and right sides in to align with the center.

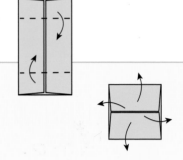

4. Fold the top half over the bottom half to create a crease in the middle, then unfold and fold the top and bottom edges to meet at the center.

5. Unfold the paper with the colored side down and fold the two side corners in to the center point.

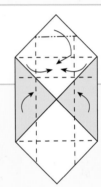

6. Fold the left and right corners of the top white diamond so the corners meet in the center point of the diamond.

7. Pull the top point of the diamond toward you, holding the left and right corners down.

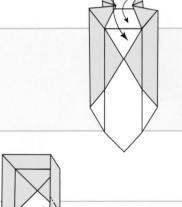

8. Push the top point down to the center as you push the left and right sides of the box outward. Tuck the top flap into the sides of the box.

9. Rotate the paper 180 degrees. Repeat steps 6, 7, and 8 with the bottom diamond.

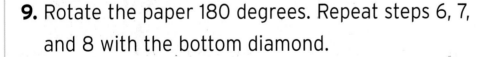

10. The four colored points should end up meeting in the center, at the bottom of the box.

Origami Photo Album

1. Fold each piece of paper in half diagonally, then unfold.	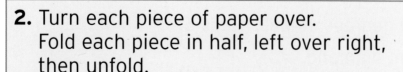
2. Turn each piece of paper over. Fold each piece in half, left over right, then unfold.	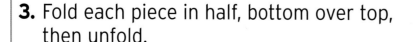
3. Fold each piece in half, bottom over top, then unfold.	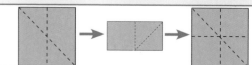

4. Turn the color B piece of paper over, so the opposite side faces you again. Place the paper so the diagonal crease runs straight up and down.

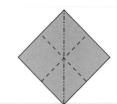

5. Place the color A paper so a 4x4 inch (10X10 cm) corner that doesn't have creases overlaps the color B paper. Do this on both sides.

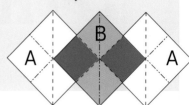

6. Glue the overlapping squares together.

7. Starting with paper A on the left, pull the top and bottom points of the square upward, so the points touch. Hold the points together at the crease and fold them over to the right, so they meet and touch the right point of the square. Fold the left point of the sqaure over to cover the other points, so you now have a folded 4x4 inch (10x10 cm) square.

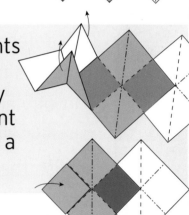

8. Repeat step 7 with the right piece of paper A.

9. Turn the entire project over and repeat step 7 with the middle piece of paper B. You should now have a stack of folded 4x4 inch (10x10 cm) squares.

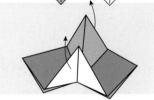

10. Lay the piece of ribbon over the top square and then glue a 4x4 inch (10x10 cm) piece of paper B over the top of it.

11. Unfold the entire project. Cut photos to fit each of the diamonds without creases. Glue the photos in place and fold the entire project back into place. Tie the ribbon to keep it closed.

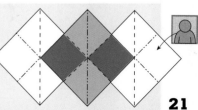

21

The Samurai Helmet

In Japan, samurai were great warriors who fought to defend their lords and land. They were famous for their undying loyalty and strict codes of honor. While samurai no longer exist, the samurai helmet remains one of the most popular origami designs in the world. The samurai helmet can even be folded using a very large sheet of paper so that you can actually wear it!

1. With the colored side face down, fold the top point down to meet the bottom point.

2. Fold the points of both sides down to meet the bottom point.

3. Fold both flaps up to meet the top point.

4. Fold the two flaps on the top layer so they point outward, as shown.

5. Fold the top layer of the bottom point up about two-thirds of the way.

6. Fold the middle strip up and fold the two outer points back.

7. Fold the bottom layer back and up.

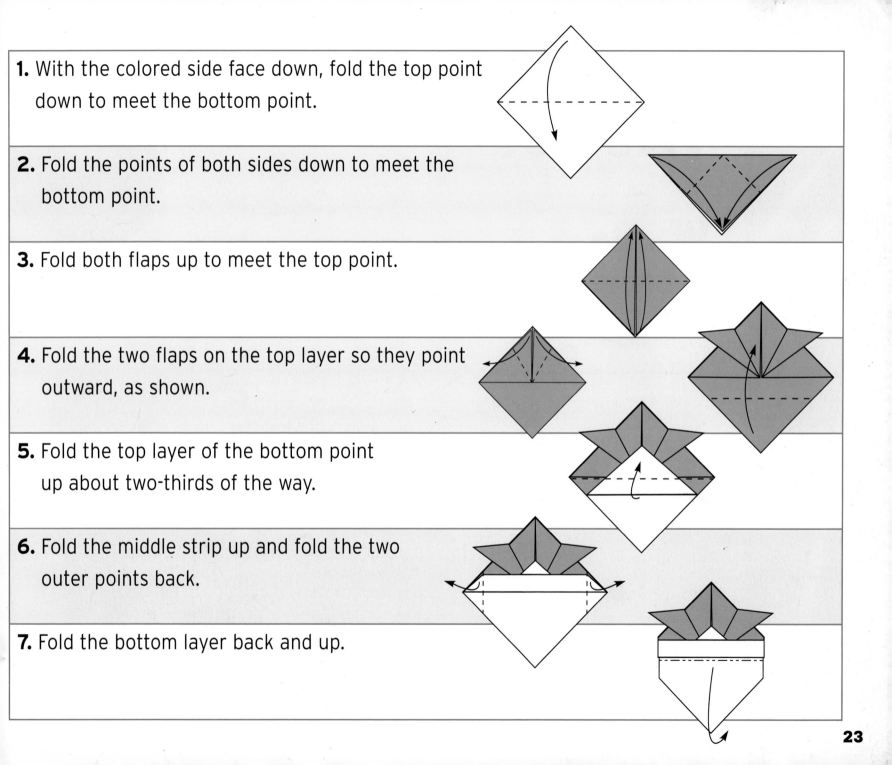

The Boat

Who hasn't folded a paper boat? This boat can float or be used to hold all kinds of small items from marbles to loose change.

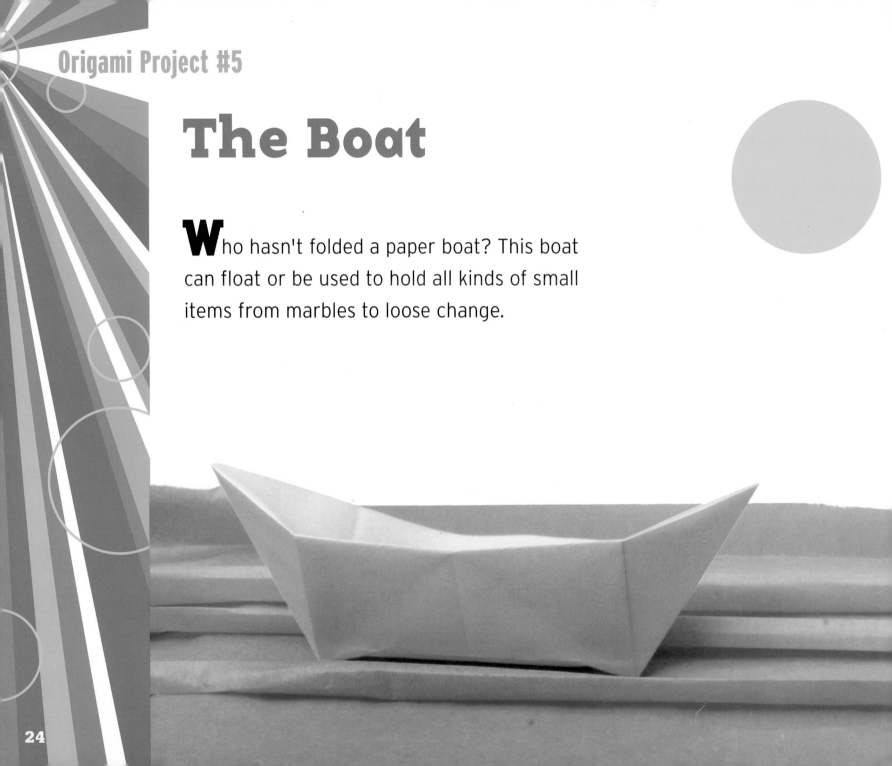

1. With the colored side down, fold the paper in half bottom over top, and in half again. Unfold the second fold.

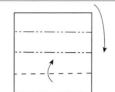

2. Fold the bottom left and bottom right points to the center crease.

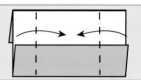

3. Fold the top layer of the top left and right points to the center crease.

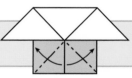

4. Fold the top layer of the top half downward.

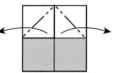

5. Pull out the two colored squares at the bottom so they form a point.

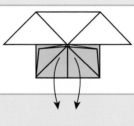

6. Pull the bottom corners of the colored side up to align with the white half.

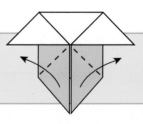

7. Open your boat. Fold the outer most points inward to the center fold. Unfold.

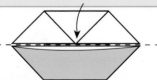

8. Flatten the bottom.

The Cicada

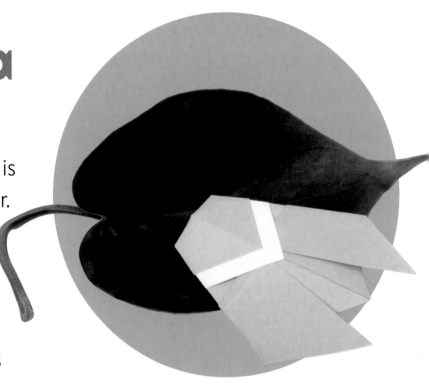

A cicada is a large insect that is often mistaken for a grasshopper. Throughout history, the cicada has fascinated people of many cultures. The male cicada is known for its lovely singing, so much so that the ancient Greeks kept caged cicadas just to hear their music. In China, the cicada symbolizes rebirth. In ancient Rome, some members of royalty wore gold cicadas in their hair.

Cicada

1. With the colored side of the paper face down, fold the top point down to meet the bottom point, then fold the side corners so they meet at the bottom point.

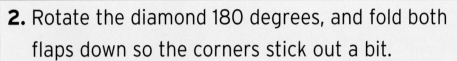

2. Rotate the diamond 180 degrees, and fold both flaps down so the corners stick out a bit.

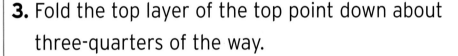

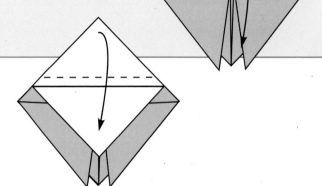

3. Fold the top layer of the top point down about three-quarters of the way.

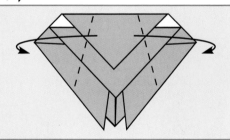

4. Fold the bottom layer of the top point over the previous fold, so a small white strip still shows.

5. Turn over and fold the sides in, so the points meet in the middle. Turn the project over again and unfold the side folds so the cicada can sit up.

Making a Scene

The more you practice, the better you become. Once you have folded enough single origami pieces, you might find that you want to do something even more exciting. What can you do with multiple origami sculptures? Make a scene.

Try folding six to eight pieces with a similar theme, such as animals or a variety of flowers. Then, using clear thread, hang them from wooden dowels or a hanger to create a mobile to hang in your window or from a ceiling.

During the holidays, get together with friends and family to create garlands of origami pieces. Simply fold all the pieces you want for the garland, then string them together using clear thread.

Animal origami works very well for scenes. Fold your animals, and create a scene using natural materials like rocks, flowers, and leaves. If you make the scene as a shadow box, hang it up for display.

Chains of Cranes

In 1797, a book called *Senbazuru Orikata* was published in Japan and gave instructions for creating groups and chains of origami cranes.

Pass the Paper

For the first thousand years of origami in Japan, folding projects were handed down from generation to generation by personal instruction. In the 17th century, origami enthusiasts started illustrating diagrams and writing instructions, usually in the form of a woodcut print.

Origami books, magazines, societies, and organizations are an important part of improving and expanding the craft. Some origami experts have published books of their original origami designs. Paper folders will always find exciting new projects by connecting with other origami hobbyists.

Some folders specialize in a certain area of origami, such as animals or complex geometric designs. For whatever you like to fold, you will have no problem finding designs that are right for you.

A Master at Work

Michael G. LaFosse has been making paper and practicing the art of paperfolding for over 40 years. He is known as one of the top origami masters in the world today. His masterpieces have been shown at the *Louvre*, in Paris, and at many other exhibitions and museums. His book, *Origamido—Masterworks of Folded Paper*, helps people understand the art of Origami. Michael and his close friend, Richard L. Alexander, own an Origami studio, *Origamido Studio*, in Haverhill, Massachusetts.

For Kids Only!

Have you created an origami piece that you're proud of and want to share with others? If so, Origami by Children is a great way to show off your work. In 1978, the nonprofit group OrigamiUSA started the traveling exhibit as a way to display kids' origami in libraries, schools, and museums across the country.

Each year, OrigamiUSA asks kids to send in their best origami. These can be traditional designs, geometrical pieces, or any other origami you can dream up. OrigamiUSA especially loves designs that kids have made up themselves.

1,000 Cranes

The Thousand Cranes Peace Network uses origami to promote peace. It has members from 24 countries including Israel, Brazil, and South Africa, and 43 states in the United States. The Network is a great way for kids to connect with each other for a common cause.

Members' names are posted on the Web site, along with how many cranes they have folded. William Rhodes of Australia has folded 3,000 cranes, and Sarah Shultis of Seattle, Washington, has 4,000. The Los Alamos Peace Project in New Mexico has folded 37,000. The kids of Nagatsuka Elementary School in Hiroshima, Japan, have folded a whopping 170,000 cranes since 1996!

In 1999, the Network sponsored the Million Paper Cranes for Peace project in which thousands of children and grown-ups from around the world participated. By 2000, they had collected nearly 1.2 million paper cranes!

No matter who you are or where you live, you can become a folder for peace.

Inspiration for Peace Cranes

Sadako Sasaki was born in Hiroshima, Japan, in 1943, two years before it was devastated by an atomic bomb. In 1955, she developed leukemia as a result of the radiation. When a friend told her the legend of how folding 1,000 paper cranes would grant her greatest wish, Sadako started folding in hopes of a longer life. By October 1955, she had folded more than 600 cranes. Sadly, she died that same month. Her classmates finished folding the rest of the cranes in her honor.

The statue of a child holding a paper crane in Hiroshima's Peace Memorial Park

Welcome to Oriland!

Paper, paper everywhere? The most fantastic origami creation ever may be "Oriland," a magical world on the Internet, of 500 people, places, and things created by Russian origami artists Yuri and Katrin Shumakov. The Shumakovs created Oriland in 2001. It is made up of eight unique kingdoms and took many years to create.

The names of the three kingdoms demonstrate the Shumakov's love of their craft: Papertown, Foldingburg, and Oriville. La Magic is one of the most popular kingdoms. It includes a tiny library, school, and 16 miniature magicians' houses. La Magic's castle is 24 inches (61 cm) high and was made with 930 sheets of paper!

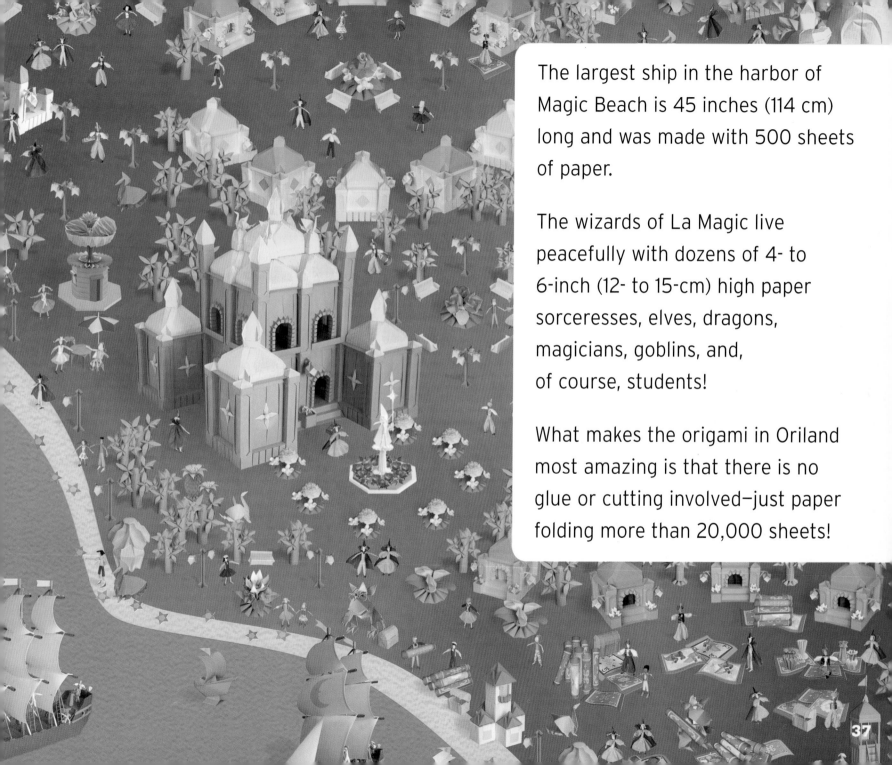

The largest ship in the harbor of Magic Beach is 45 inches (114 cm) long and was made with 500 sheets of paper.

The wizards of La Magic live peacefully with dozens of 4- to 6-inch (12- to 15-cm) high paper sorceresses, elves, dragons, magicians, goblins, and, of course, students!

What makes the origami in Oriland most amazing is that there is no glue or cutting involved—just paper folding more than 20,000 sheets!

It's All in the Math!

You might not be a mathematician, but you should know that origami is based on principles of math and geometry. When you create any fold, you are making a geometrical shape—a rectangle, a triangle, a polygon, a square, and so on. So believe it or not, when you are creating origami, you're doing math.

Many folding artists like to challenge themselves with difficult projects that require a strong understanding of geometry. These projects are often called mathematical origami, geometrical origami, or complex origami. Complex origami pieces often look like science models, such as that of an atom or a molecule. Sometimes these projects are many folded pieces assembled together into one large sculpture.

Who's Made History in Origami?

Akira Yoshizawa

Akira Yoshizawa of Japan is considered the master of modern origami. Although he started out life as a factory worker, by 1937 he had dedicated his life to the study and further development of origami. Yoshizawa standardized origami diagrams. The folding systems he created are used all around the world.

Although he created more than 50,000 original origami designs during his lifetime, only a few hundred of them were published in books.

He lived to be 94 years old and died on March 14, 2005, which happened to be his birthday.

Akira Yoshizawa

Yuri and Katrin Shumakov

Yuri and Katrin Shumakov

This origami-obsessed Russian couple, Yuri and Katrin Shumakov, are superstars of the paper folding world, known for their magical paper kingdoms called Oriland. They have written several origami books and instructional CDs, and their work has been displayed in many countries including the United States, Russia, and Singapore.

Both Yuri and Katrin are psychologists who have studied how origami helps children learn. Their scientific research shows that by doing origami, kids develop better use of both hands, whether they are left- or right-handed. They also discovered that origami can improve creativity and intelligence in children ages 7 to 11.

Yuri and Katrin believe that origami is "entertainment for the soul, gymnastics for the mind, and training for the hands."

41

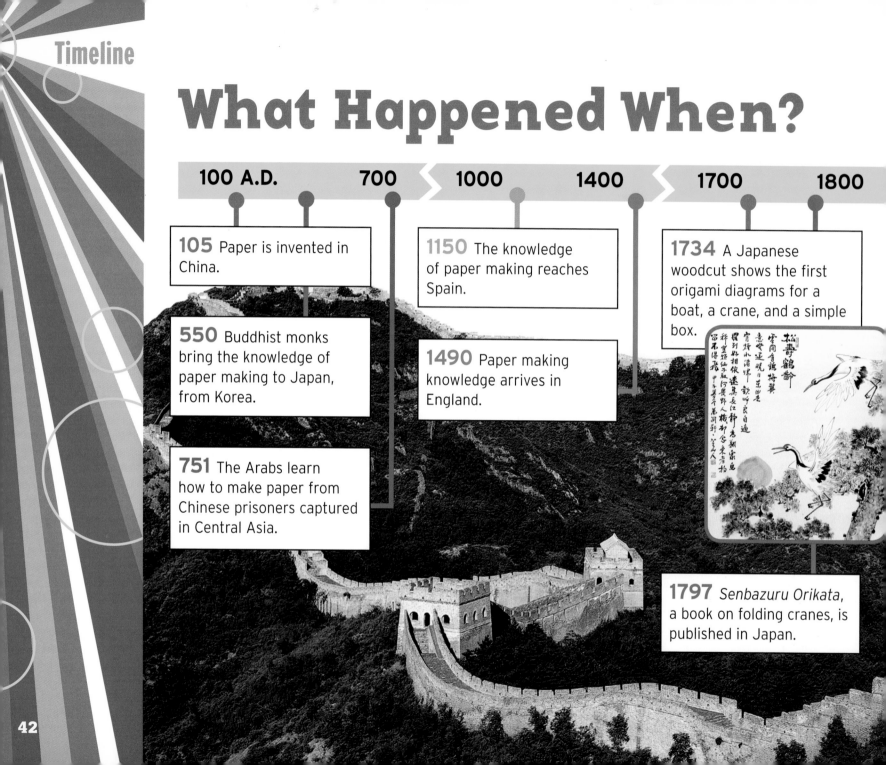

What Happened When?

| 100 A.D. | | 700 | 1000 | 1400 | 1700 | 1800 |

105 Paper is invented in China.

1150 The knowledge of paper making reaches Spain.

1734 A Japanese woodcut shows the first origami diagrams for a boat, a crane, and a simple box.

550 Buddhist monks bring the knowledge of paper making to Japan, from Korea.

1490 Paper making knowledge arrives in England.

751 The Arabs learn how to make paper from Chinese prisoners captured in Central Asia.

1797 *Senbazuru Orikata*, a book on folding cranes, is published in Japan.

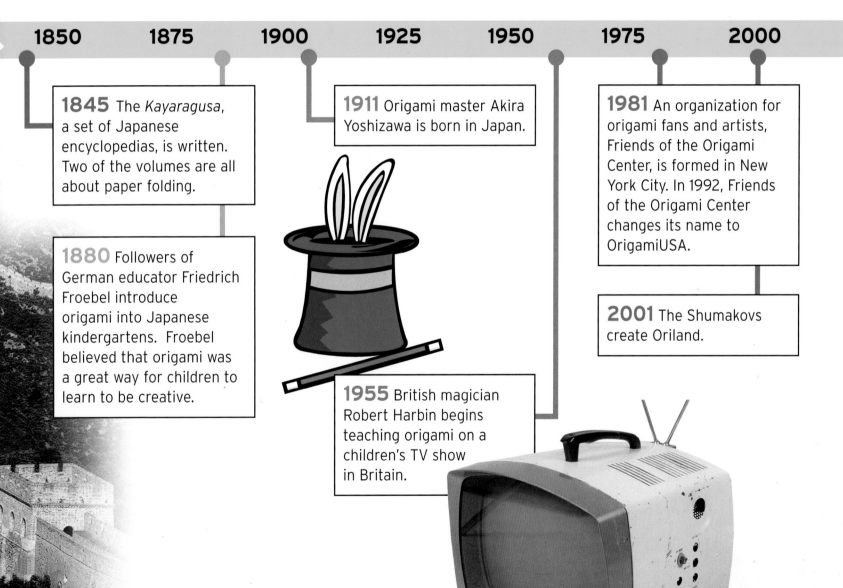

1850 **1875** **1900** **1925** **1950** **1975** **2000**

1845 The *Kayaragusa*, a set of Japanese encyclopedias, is written. Two of the volumes are all about paper folding.

1880 Followers of German educator Friedrich Froebel introduce origami into Japanese kindergartens. Froebel believed that origami was a great way for children to learn to be creative.

1911 Origami master Akira Yoshizawa is born in Japan.

1955 British magician Robert Harbin begins teaching origami on a children's TV show in Britain.

1981 An organization for origami fans and artists, Friends of the Origami Center, is formed in New York City. In 1992, Friends of the Origami Center changes its name to OrigamiUSA.

2001 The Shumakovs create Oriland.

Fun Origami Facts

Movie star Renee Zellweger wore an origami-inspired gown to the 76th annual Academy awards in 2004. The white silk dress was designed by Carolina Herrera and had a large origami bow at the back.

The blintz base gets its name from a folding method used to make blintzes, a type of pancake.

In 1922, the famous magician and escape artist Harry Houdini wrote a book called *Paper Magic* that included instructions for folding the flapping bird.

During the mid-1930s, attendees at a magicians' convention in Chicago wore rings that were folded dollars.

The world's largest crane was folded by 1,000 people in Odate City, Japan, in January 2001. It had a wingspan of 256½ feet (78 m)!

In the early 1970s, origami artist Lillian Oppenheimer wrote a book called *Folding Paper Puppets* with puppeteer Shari Lewis, who hosted her own TV show starring a puppet called Lamb Chop.

Modern day napkin folding has its roots in origami. Large cloth napkins can be folded into shapes of animals, fruits, and boats.

Origami Words to Know

base: a simple series of folds that forms the start of an origami design

cicada: an origami design modeled on the cicada, an insect that resembles a locust

complex origami: difficult origami designs often involving many sheets of paper

crane: a classic origami design of the bird

fish: an origami base

irogami: origami paper that is colored on one side and white on the other

kite: an origami base

masu box: a simple, folded paper box, modeled on small wooden boxes used in Japan to measure rice or beans

mountain fold: a fold in which the paper is folded away from you with the white side facing out

origami: Japanese word for "paper folding;" the art of paper folding

samurai helmet: a popular origami design

stationery: paper that is usually used for writing letters

valley fold: a fold in which the paper is folded toward you with the colored side facing out

GLOSSARY
Other Words to Know

botany: the study of plants

culture: group of people who share beliefs, customs, and a way of life.

elite: the wealthy upper class of a society

enthusiast: someone who gets very excited about a certain hobby or interest

exception: going against the norm or the rules

intricate: complicated, with a great deal of detail

Where To Learn More

At the Library

Kashahara, Kunihiko. *Extreme Origami*. New York: Sterling Publishing, 2003.

Lang, Robert J. *Origami in Action: Paper Toys That Fly, Flap, Gobble, and Inflate*. New York: St. Martin's Griffin, 1997.

On the Road

OrigamiUSA
15 W. 77th St.
New York, NY 10024-5192
212/769-563

ON THE WEB

For more information on ORIGAMI use FactHound to track down Web sites related to this book.

1. Go to www.facthound.com
2. Type in this book ID: 0756516897
3. Click on the *Fetch It* button.

Your trusty FactHound will fetch the best Web sites for you!

INDEX

Base forms, 14-15
 kite, fish
Boat, 24-25

Cicada, 26-27
Complex origami, 38
Cranes, 34-35

Diagrams, 10-11

Folding Paper Puppets, 45
Folds, 12-13
mountain, valley, petal,
 rabbit ear, squash, crimp,
 pleat, sink, inside reverse,
 outside reverse
Froebel, Frederick, 43

Garlands, 28-29

Harbin, Robert, 43
Houdini, Harry, 44

Kayaragusa, 43

LaFosse, Michael G., 31

Masu box, 18-19

Oppenheimer, Lillian, 45
OrigamiUSA, 32

Oriland, 36-37

Papers, 8-9

Photo Album, 20-21

Samurai helmet, 22-23
Sasaki, Sadako, 35
Scenes, 28-29
Senbazuru Orikata, 29
Shamakov, Yuri and Katrin,
 36, 41, 43
Snake, 16-17

Thousand Cranes Peace
Network, 34-35

Yoshizawa, Akira, 40, 43

About the Author

Thiranut Deborah Berry spent much of her childhood living between Bangkok and Tokyo, where she developed an early love of origami, sushi, and Hello Kitty. She works as a writer, editor, and art director in children's publishing and lives in New York City.